OUTSIDE THE DOOR

John McInnes, *Senior Author*

John Ryckman

NELSON CANADA

© Nelson Canada,
A Division of International Thomson Limited, 1986

All rights in this book are reserved

Published in 1986 by
Nelson Canada,
A Division of International Thomson Limited
1120 Birchmount Road
Scarborough, Ontario
M1K 5G4

ISBN 0-17-602350-X

Canadian Cataloguing in Publication Data

McInnes, John, 1927-
   Outside the Door

(Networks)
ISBN 0-17-602350-X

I. Readers (Primary). I. Ryckman, John, 1928-
II. Title. III. Series: Networks (Toronto, Ont.)

PE1119.M2558 1985   428.6   C85-099478-0

Printed and bound in Canada

Contents

A Brand New Day

The sun woke me up this morning.
The sunlight seemed to say,
    Be sunny and bright
    From morning till night,
    For today is a brand new day.

I looked at myself in the mirror.
The mirror seemed to say,
    I smile at you
    When you're smiling too,
    For today is a brand new day.

I heard a bluejay calling.
The bluejay seemed to say,
    Come out and have fun
    In the snow, in the sun,
    For today is a brand new day.

My puppy bounced around me.
His big eyes seemed to say,
   There's a world to explore
   Outside the door,
   For today is a brand new day.

Yesterday Was Different

Every day, at four o'clock,
I take my puppy for a walk.

But yesterday was different.

Yesterday I took my puppy for his shots.

Every day, at four o'clock,
I have peanut butter cookies.

But yesterday was different.

Yesterday I had chocolate chip cookies.

Every day, at four o'clock,
I go to see my grandma.

But yesterday was different.

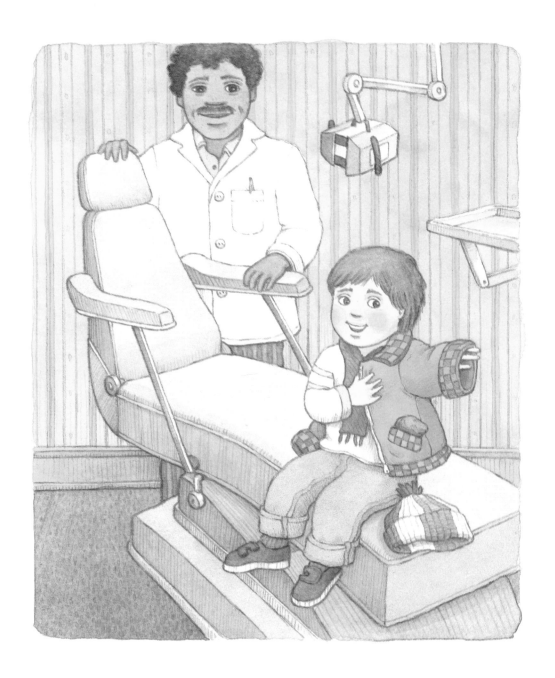

Yesterday I went to see the dentist.

Every day, at four o'clock,
I play hockey on the driveway
with my brother.

But yesterday was different.

Yesterday we played hockey in the house.

Every day, at four o'clock,
I help my mom make dinner.

But yesterday was different.

Yesterday we all went out for pizza.
Yum, yum, yum!
Yesterday was really different!

I Love Winter

by Clara Juh Lewis

I love winter! Winter is cold.
It's Christmas with sleds.
It's warm snuggly beds.

It's silver snowflakes.
It's skaters on lakes.
It's snowmen that stand
In a snowy, white land.

It's bluejays that feed
On sunflower seed.
It's angels that pose
In wintertime clothes.

It's a polka-dot sky.
It's winter. That's why...
I love winter.

A Very Special Day

On Monday Mrs. Chan asked,
"What's special about today?"

"I know," said Robert. "Today is the day
they put up the boards for our skating rink."

"That's right," said Mrs. Chan.
"That's what's special about today."

On Tuesday Mrs. Chan asked,
"What's special about today?"

"I know," said Anne-Marie. "Today is the day
they put up the lights on our skating rink."

"That's right," said Mrs. Chan.
"That's what's special about today."

On Wednesday Mrs. Chan asked,
"What's special about today?"

"I know," said Andrew. "Today is the day
they flood our skating rink."

"That's right," said Mrs. Chan.
"That's what's special about today."

On Thursday Mrs. Chan asked,
"What's special about today?"

"I know," said Mary-Jo. "Today is the day
they flood our skating rink again."

"That's right," said Mrs. Chan.
"That's what's special about today."

On Friday Mrs. Chan asked,
"What's *very* special about today?"

"I know," said Ivan.
"Today is the day we go skating
on our skating rink."

"That's right," said Mrs. Chan.
"That's what's *very* special about today."

"Yeah!" said all the children.

Hurry Straight Home

On Monday, when school was over,
Mrs. Chan said, "Goodbye, girls and boys.
And remember, hurry straight home.
Don't dawdle on the way."

On Monday Billy forgot.

He stopped to catch
a snowflake.

He stopped to slide
on the ice.

He stopped to make his name
in the snow.

On Monday Billy got home late.

On Tuesday, when school was over,
Mrs. Chan said, "Goodbye, girls and boys.
And remember, hurry straight home.
Don't dawdle on the way."

On Tuesday Billy forgot.

He stopped to watch
a snowplow.

He stopped to jump
in a snowbank.

He stopped to make tracks
in the snow.

On Tuesday Billy got home late.

On Wednesday, when school was over,
Mrs. Chan said, "Goodbye, girls and boys.
And remember, hurry straight home.
Don't dawdle on the way."

On Wednesday Billy forgot.

He stopped to help Mrs. Macdonald brush snow off her car.

He stopped to help Mr. Garcia shovel snow off his walk.

On Wednesday Billy got home late.

On Thursday, when school was over,
Mrs. Chan said, "Goodbye, girls and boys.
And remember, hurry straight home.
Don't dawdle on the way."

On Thursday Billy forgot.

He stopped to build
a snowman.

He stopped to knock icicles
off a fence.

He stopped to throw snowballs
at a tree.

On Thursday Billy got home late.

On Friday, when school was over,
Mrs. Chan said, "Goodbye, girls and boys.
And remember, hurry straight home.
Don't dawdle on the way."

On Friday Billy remembered.

He remembered to hurry
straight home from school.
He remembered not to dawdle.
He remembered that tonight was the night
he was going to get a new pair of skates!

A Bad Cold

by Carolann Reynolds

A sneeze—*atchoo!*
A sneeze—*atchoo!*
I've got to sneeze
a sneeze— *aaatchoo!*
It's bursting my zipper.
It blew off my slipper.
My nose is a dripper. . . .
Atchoo! —sniff, sniff.

Atchoo! Atchoo!

Chelsea was getting ready for school.
All at once she sneezed, "Atchoo! Atchoo!"
Then she sneezed again, "Atchoo! Atchoo!"

"Chelsea," said her father, "you have a cold. You'll have to stay home today."

Chelsea's mother said, "Go back to bed, Chelsea."

"Atchoo! Atchoo!" sneezed Chelsea.

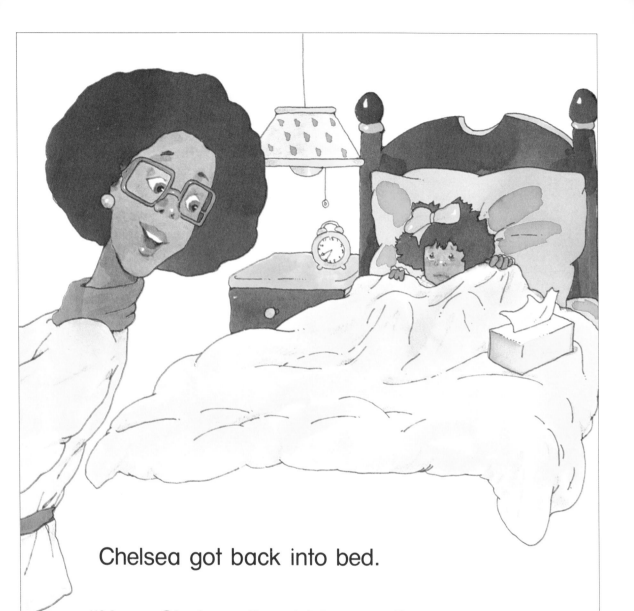

Chelsea got back into bed.

"Now, Chelsea," said her mother,
"I'm going downstairs
 to make some hot lemonade for you.
 You stay in bed and keep warm."

"Atchoo! Atchoo!" sneezed Chelsea.

Chelsea drank the hot lemonade.

"Now, Chelsea," said her mother,
"try to go to sleep.
I'm going back downstairs."

Chelsea tried to go to sleep,
but she couldn't.

"Mommy," she called, "I'm bored."

Chelsea's mother brought her a puzzle.
"Now, Chelsea," said her mother,
"play with your puzzle
and then try to go to sleep.
I'm going back downstairs."

Chelsea played with her puzzle.
Then she tried to go to sleep,
but she couldn't.

"Mommy," she called, "I'm bored."

Chelsea's mother brought her a book.
"Now, Chelsea," said her mother,
"read your book and then try to go to sleep.
I'm going back downstairs."

Chelsea read her book.
Then she tried to go to sleep,
but she couldn't.

"Mommy," she called, "I'm bored."

Chelsea's mother brought her a sandwich.
"Now, Chelsea," said her mother,
"eat your sandwich, play with your puppets,
and then try to go to sleep.
I'm going back downstairs."

Chelsea ate her sandwich
and played with her puppets.
Then she tried to go to sleep,
but she couldn't.

"Mommy," she called, "I'm bored."

All day long Chelsea's mother
brought her things.

Chelsea ate ice cream
and she played with her toys.
Then she tried to go to sleep,
but she couldn't.

At five o'clock Chelsea's father came home.
He went upstairs to see her.
"Did you stay in bed?" he asked.
"Did you keep warm?
Did you have a good sleep?"

Chelsea said, "I drank hot lemonade,
I played with a puzzle,
I read a book, I ate a sandwich,
I played with my puppets, I ate ice cream,
and I played with my toys.
Then I tried to go to sleep,
but I couldn't."

"How is your cold?" asked Chelsea's father.

Chelsea didn't answer.
She was sound asleep.

Good Morning to Me

(Dragon comes in, singing loudly.)

DRAGON: Good morning to me.
            Good morning to me.
            Good morning, good morning,
            Good morning to me.

BOX: Snore! Snore!

DRAGON: I know that snore. It's Rosie.
           She's asleep in the box.
           I won't wake her up.
           I will go away and come back later.

(*Dragon goes out, singing softly*.)

DRAGON: Good morning to me...

(Rosie comes in, singing loudly.)

ROSIE: Good morning to me.
Good morning to me.
Good morning, good morning,
Good morning to me.

BOX: Snore! Snore!

ROSIE: I know that snore. It's Dragon.
He's asleep in the box.
I won't wake him up.
I will go away and come back later.

(Rosie goes out, singing softly.)

ROSIE: Good morning to me...

(Dragon comes back in, singing softly.)

DRAGON: Good morning to me...

BOX: Snore! Snore!

DRAGON: Rosie's still asleep.
I will sit here and wait for her
to wake up.

(Dragon sits down.)

(Rosie comes back in, singing softly.)

ROSIE: Good morning to me…

BOX: Snore! Snore!

ROSIE: Dragon's still asleep.
            I will sit here and wait for him
            to wake up.

*(Rosie sits down on the other side
of the box.)*

DRAGON: I'm tired of waiting.
I'm going to wake Rosie up.
ROSIE! ROSIE! WAKE UP!

ROSIE: I'm not asleep.

BOX: Snore! Snore!

DRAGON: You *are* asleep.
I can hear you snoring.

BOX: Snore! Snore!

ROSIE: That's not me snoring.
That's *you* snoring.

BOX: Snore! Snore!

DRAGON: That's not me snoring. I'm awake.

BOX: Snore! Snore!

ROSIE: If it isn't you and it isn't me,
then who is snoring in the box?

BOX:	It's *me* snoring.
DRAGON:	Who are you?
BOX:	I'm B.J. Penguin. Open the box. Help me get out of here!

(Dragon and Rosie open the box. B.J. jumps out.)

(B.J. bows to Rosie and Dragon.)

B.J.:   Who are you?

ROSIE: I'm Rosie Raccoon.

DRAGON: I'm Dragon.

B.J.:   Where am I?

DRAGON: You're here.

B.J.:   Where's here?

ROSIE: You're in Mrs. Chan's classroom.

B.J.:   Good! This is just where I want to be.

DRAGON:	Can you sing? Do you know any songs?
ROSIE:	Do you know "Good Morning to Me"?
B.J.:	No, I don't know that song, but I know another one.
DRAGON:	What song do you know?
B.J.:	"The More We Get Together."

ROSIE: Good! We know that song too.
           Let's sing it together.

DRAGON: Let's all sing it!

           (*Everyone sings*.)

EVERYONE: The more we get together,
           together, together,
           The more we get together,
           the happier we'll be. . . .

Not Bad at All!

Dragon was playing in the snow.
He took a little ball of snow
and rolled it on the ground.
The snowball got bigger and bigger.

Just then Rosie Raccoon came along.
She saw the big snowball.

"Dragon," she asked,
"what are you going to do
with that big snowball?"

"I'm going to make a snow penguin,"
said Dragon.

"I can help," said Rosie.
"What do you want me to do?"

"Make another snowball," said Dragon.
"Make a small one."

Rosie took a little ball of snow.
She rolled it on the ground.

"Is this snowball okay?" asked Rosie.

"Yes," said Dragon, "it's just right."

Dragon and Rosie put the small snowball
on top of the big one.

"Is it finished?" asked Rosie.

"It's not finished yet," said Dragon.
"It needs two eyes and a nose."

"Okay," said Rosie. "You get the eyes
and I will get the nose."

Dragon found two stones.
"These will make good eyes," he said.

Dragon put the eyes on the penguin.

Rosie found a carrot.
"This will make a good nose," she said.

Rosie put the nose on the penguin.

"Is it finished now?" asked Rosie.

"Yes," said Dragon.
"How do you like our snow penguin?"

"It's not bad," said Rosie.
"It's not bad at all!"

Just then B.J. Penguin came along.

"How do you like our snow penguin?"
asked Dragon.

"It's not bad," said B.J.
"It's not bad at all!
Now you come and see
what I have made."

"Guess what it is," said B.J.

"It looks a little bit like a dragon,"
said Dragon.

"It looks a little bit like a raccoon,"
said Rosie. "What is it?"

"It's a *dracoon*," said B.J.
"How do you like it?"

"It's not bad," said Dragon.
"It's not bad at all!"

"It's very, very good," said Rosie.
"It's the best dracoon I have ever seen!"

Penguins Everywhere

There's a penguin on the table.
There's a penguin on the chair.
There's a penguin eating popcorn.
There are penguins everywhere!

There's a penguin on the ladder.
There's a penguin on the ground.
There's a penguin on the rooftop.
There are penguins all around!

There's a penguin in the mirror.
There's a penguin next to me.
There are penguins everywhere I look
That only I can see!

All About Penguins

Penguins live near the South Pole.
They are birds, but they cannot fly.
They can swim and they can walk.
But they swim much better than they walk.

Penguins find all their food
in the sea.
They eat fish and *krill*.
A krill is a tiny shellfish.

Penguins build their nests on the ground.
The mother and father
dig a shallow hole with their feet.
The mother and father
put some stones in the hole.
Now the nest is ready.

The mother penguin
lays one or two eggs in the nest.
The father and the mother penguins
take turns keeping the eggs warm.

In a few weeks the eggs hatch,
and the baby penguins come out.
Baby penguins are called *chicks*.

The chicks are covered
with soft feathers called *down*.
The down keeps them warm.

The mother and the father penguins
take turns feeding the chicks.
One parent watches over the chicks.
The other parent goes to find food.
The penguin chicks grow quickly.

The mother and the father penguins
teach the little penguins to swim, dive,
and catch food.

When fall comes,
the penguins leave the South Pole.
They go north to find food
in warmer waters.

When spring comes,
the penguins go back
to the South Pole.

Through the Deep Snow

Part One: Where's Barney?

Terry, Jake, and Grandmother
were alone in the farmhouse.
Outside it was snowing and blowing.
But inside the big farm kitchen,
it was safe and warm.

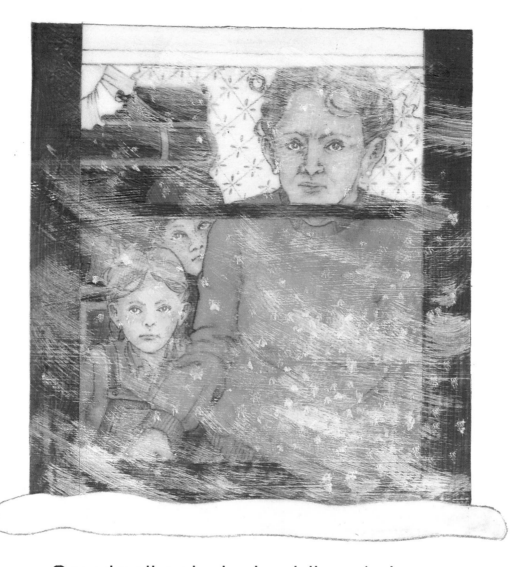

Grandmother looked out the window.
"This is the worst storm of the winter,"
she said. "But we'll be safe in here.
We have wood for the fire and lots to eat.
We won't have to go outside
until the morning."

Just then Jake said, "Where's Barney?"

"He's around here someplace,"
said Grandmother. "Here, Barney!"
she called.

"Barney! Barney!" called Terry.

But the little dog didn't come.

"Come on, Terry," said Jake.
"Let's find Barney."

Terry and Jake looked everywhere
in the big farmhouse.
They couldn't find Barney.
They called and called,
"Barney! Barney!"

But the little dog didn't come.

"Grandmother," said Jake,
"Barney isn't in the house.
 He must be outside!"

Terry began to cry. "Barney's lost,"
she sobbed. "He's lost in the storm.
We'll never see him again!"

"Now, Terry," said Grandmother, "don't cry.
 Barney isn't lost. He must be outside."

Grandmother opened the kitchen door.
"Barney! Barney!" she called.
"Here, Barney!"

But the little dog didn't come.

Grandmother called again, "Barney! Barney!"

"Listen," said Jake.

"I hear him!" said Terry.

"I can hear him too," said Grandmother.
"He must be in the barn."

"Why doesn't he come when we call him?"
asked Terry.

"The snow is too deep," said Grandmother.
"If he tried to come,
he might get lost in the snow."

"We'll have to go and get him,"
said Jake.

Part Two: Step by Step

Terry, Jake, and Grandmother got ready
to go outside. Grandmother got a long rope.
Jake got a flashlight.

"We'll have to be very careful,"
said Grandmother.
"We don't want to get lost in the snow."

Grandmother tied one end
of the rope to a post.
She tied the other end around her.

"Hang on to the rope," she said,
"and don't let go."

Step.....by.....step
they walked through the deep snow.

At last they came to the barn.

Inside the barn,
the little dog was waiting for them.

"Barney! Barney!" cried Terry.
"We found you!"

Barney was happy to see them.
He barked and jumped and danced around.

"Now," said Grandmother,
"we have to get back to the house.
Jake, you carry Barney.
Terry can carry the flashlight.
And remember, hang on to the rope
and don't let go."

Step.....by.....step
they walked through the deep snow.

At last they came to the house.

Grandmother gave Barney his dinner.
Then they all sat down by the fire.

Outside it was snowing and blowing.
But inside the big farm kitchen,
it was safe and warm.

Project Manager: Christine Anderson
Editor: Jocelyn Van Huyse
Design and Art Direction: Rob McPhail
Associate Designer: Lorraine Tuson
Cover Design: Taylor/Levkoe Associates Limited
Cover Illustration: Vlasta Van Kampen
Typesetting: Trigraph Inc.
Printing: The Bryant Press Limited

Acknowledgements

All selections in this book have been written or adapted by John McInnes and John Ryckman, with the exception of the following:

I Love Winter by Clara Juh Lewis. Copyright © 1965 by James and Clara Marie Lewis.

A Bad Cold by Carolann Reynolds. Reprinted by permission of the author.

Illustrations

Barry Carlton and Elva Hook: 34; Brenda Clark: 58-68; Hélène Desputeaux: 18-23; Eugenie Fernandés: 4-5; Linda Hendry: 24-33; Vesna Krystanovich: 35-45, 46-57; Alan Moak: 16-17; Roger Paré: 69-71; Debi Perna: 6-15; Vlasta Van Kampen: 82-95

Photographs

Jen and Des Bartlett/Bruce Coleman Limited: 74; Julie and Jim Bruton/Ardea London: 80-81; Inigo Everson/Bruce Coleman Limited: 73 (top); Clem Haagner/Ardea London: 72-73 (bottom), 79; Jeremy Jones: 34; Edwin Mickleburgh/Ardea London: 76, 77, 78; Bernard Stonehouse/Ardea London: 75

4567890 BP 21098